83

115

Bn.

Vlc. Db.

Tutti

118

Adagio

Anthem II
Let thy hand be strengthened
No. 1

FOUR CORONATION ANTHEMS

G. F. HANDEL

Anthem I

Zadok the priest

Printed in Great Britain

OXFORD UNIVERSITY PRESS, MUSIC DEPARTMENT, GREAT CLARENDON STREET, OXFORD OX2 6DP

No. 2

No. 3

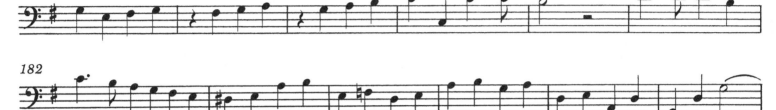

Anthem III
The King shall rejoice
No. 1

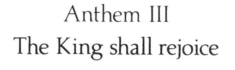

No. 2

* Throughout this movement, both ♪♪ and ♪·♪ may be performed ♪♪.

128

135

140

146

152

160

166

172

178

184

No. 3

A tempo giusto. Non tanto allegro

190

Adagio   **Allegro**

195

203

Senza Db.

211

Tutti

220

230

239

250

261
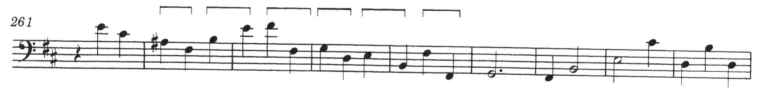

270

281

No. 4

Anthem IV
My heart is inditing
No. 1

No. 2

No. 3

147   **Andante**

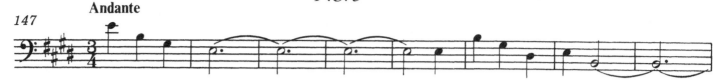

155

162

170

179

188

195

201

209   Senza Db.

218   Tutti

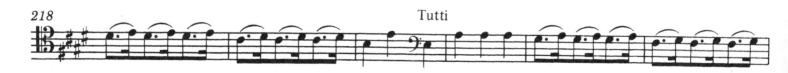

No. 4

Allegro e staccato

279

283

287

291

295

299

303

307

311

315   **Adagio**

ISBN 978-0-19-335272-8

Reproduced and printed by
Halstan & Co. Ltd., Amersham, Bucks., England